Taking the L

Words for Liberation

Latrina Kelly-James

Taking The L

Words for Liberation

gatekeeper press

Columbus, Ohio

The views and opinions expressed in this book are solely those of the author and do not reflect the views or opinions of Gatekeeper Press. Gatekeeper Press is not to be held responsible for and expressly disclaims responsibility of the content herein.

Taking the L: Words for Liberation

Published by Gatekeeper Press
2167 Stringtown Rd, Suite 109
Columbus, OH 43123-2989
www.GatekeeperPress.com

Copyright © 2022 by Latrina Kelly-James
All rights reserved. Neither this book, nor any parts within it may be sold or reproduced in any form or by any electronic or mechanical means, including information storage and retrieval systems, without permission in writing from the author. The only exception is by a reviewer, who may quote short excerpts in a review.

The editorial work for this book is entirely the product of the author. Gatekeeper Press did not participate in and is not responsible for any aspect of this element.

Library of Congress Control Number: 2022938652

ISBN (paperback): 9781662924910
eISBN: 9781662924927

FOR US…

Contents

A Message from Oya 1

Minneapolis May 25, 2020 3
Whiteness Is Burning: From Black Wall Street to
    Minneapolis, Our Souls Will Be Free 4

When you enter me 7
Bad Language 8
Direct Action 10
For Him 11
Be My Peace 12
Emasculation 13
Doormat 14
When He Hurts 15

Nurturing the Nature of Our Children is Revolutionary. 17
Our Babies 18
A Black Mother's Love 21
Girls Who Know 23
What Did I Do? My #Blackmommymagic
    and Overexposing My Babies to Racism 24
Generational Wealth 28
The Great Migration 29

Being 34
Growth 35
Toni Transitions (For the Queen Toni Morrison) 36
Living 38

On Resiliency 39
Naked... 41
She's Here 42
You've Lamented, Now Be Free: An Open Letter to
   All My Peeps on Your Constructed Doom's Day
   (Obama Farewell)...and for Today. 43
Haiku for All That Is Burning 47
Crisis KRST COVID 48
Audacity 50
on the ascension of bell hooks 51
They Keep Coming for Us............................. 54

A Message from Oya

Our joy rests
Deep under our skin
Muffled by grief
Stifled in trauma
Swimming in old blood
Mixed with the salt of
Atlantic Ocean waters

My dears
Wake yourselves
to rest
With each breath
In each moment of rest
that your ancestors could not take
Laugh
Weave in the laughter
in the midst of your pain

Light a candle for your futures
Say a prayer to get you through today
Be patient with yourself
with our people
Speak life into every single thing

Peel back your layers of hurt
Cleanse in your tears
wipe your slate clean

Sit
Feel us
beneath your skin
Urging to breakthrough
Remember you
Remember you
Oh sweet children

Remember us
We hear
We are here
For you
Conjure joy my dears

Sincerely,
Your ancestors

Minneapolis May 25, 2020

Let
it
burn

Whiteness Is Burning: From Black Wall Street to Minneapolis, Our Souls Will Be Free

Originally published on May 31, 2020 on the remembrance of...

May 31, 1921: Black Wall Street, an all Black American, economically independent community, was set on fire by White supremacists who believed a Black man, Dick Rowland, raped a White woman.

Ninety-nine years later to the date, May 31, 2020, this entire land burns. It burns because George Floyd was lynched right before our eyes. It burns because Breona Taylor was shot while she was sleeping. For me, it sent an unrecognizable, but familiar sensation through my veins. I could remember all of those lynched before me, monogrammed in my blood. America is burning because we have realized the depth of violence and daily harm this country inflicts on Black people, to maintain its true mission: Whiteness.

The United States of America is built on manifest destiny—the belief that the expansion of America was justified and inevitable. While colonization wreaked genocide on indigenous people across the western hemisphere, and pillaged its natural beauty for capitalist gain, this land's colonization included all of the above. *But, its goal was to create a land of sovereignty for the White man.* Anything that threatens that is subject to violence and annihilation.

We must deeply understand that the fulfillment of this destiny is rooted in the necessity of Black people as in service to White people. It was justified through slavery, and is justified through incarcerating more humans than anywhere else in the world, then forcing them to produce for the sake of capitalism. Fulfillment was justified through diminishing the femininity of Black women to uterine workhorses, only fit to produce human capital.

Manifest destiny means that states decide to reopen at the same time data says that Black people are dying of COVID at higher rates. It means testing vaccines at hospitals in communities with high Black populations with no warning or explanations. Fulfillment is justified through loving Black culture and crushing Black people. The moment any Black person steps outside of service to Whiteness, our bodies are at risk; our necks are literally stepped on and crushed.

It is a reflex. That woman in Central Park would not dare be corrected by a Black man. She is the protected one. Her reflex was to call her people…the police. Her reflex sought to put Christopher Cooper in his place; to remind him whose land he was standing on. That reflex is rooted in blood memory and kitchen table conversations with language White people were never emboldened to say in public, until now.

Violence and dehumanization of Black people is the secret sauce of America's democracy. The casual anti-Blackness has also meant that anyone in proximity to Blackness is at risk of getting used for the purposes of Whiteness, whether it's working the land to put food on America's table, and then being deported for taking up too much space. Capitalism and its Whiteness can't exist without Black people and racism.

Black Wall Street burned 99 years this month because the thought of White supremacy's most prized possession, the White women, coupled with the economic independence of Black people, no longer in service to Whiteness, threatened the literal foundations of this system. The inevitable expansion of and control by the White man was at risk of annihilation.

America burns today because we are no longer asking or strategizing on how to fix something that isn't broken. America burns because we know the system is working for its true purpose: the justification and inevitability of Whiteness and White prosperity at all costs.

America burns today because we, Black people, have a deep blood memory too. We are downloading our ancestral power. We are not in service to anyone else but the spirit of our ancestors and our children. Black people, now is the time to move further towards liberation in practice. Succeed and thrive on our own terms. Release our reliance on systems and move towards our interdependence on one another. Collectivism birthed Wall Street. Our reliance on this system to give us freedom, respect or humanity has ended.

I see you my people—from our ancestors in Tulsa, to all of us standing in grief in Minneapolis and across this country. Uplift and support all of those folks who've been covering and sustaining our communities for decades. The people that have been intervening before conflict happens—eliminating our need for police; the healing of doulas and midwives who birthed almost all of my aunts and uncles; the mutual aid organizing to bail people out, asking for nothing in return; those bringing food to our elders to whom COVID has left bare. They have the blueprint. They need investment. Grieve, scream, cry, drink your water, get aligned, hold one another tight. I feel the shift. Strap up for the journey. We will get there. *Ase.*

> *"For a people to survive in struggle it must be on its own terms: The collective wisdom which is the synthesis of culture and the experience of that struggle. The shared past is precious, not for itself but because it is the basis of consciousness, of knowing, of being."* Cedric Robinson

When you enter me
please be cleansed in truth
for you will live in me forever

Bad Language

Resiliency
Can kiss my ass
It's a bad word
Rooted in my pain
My exploitation
It says…you can take it
Just take a breath

I say
It's the bad word
On the list my momma taught me

I say
It's killing me to heal
To spring back
To self-care

I wanna just
Dance without boundaries
Cry joy tears
Not feel the memories of torture in my veins

Every piece of ancestral land I touch
Send pings through my skin
Up my veins
Into the ventricles
Synapses to my brain

And then
I remember
It all

And I am forced to bathe in it
Wash it off of my skin
With coffee cane sugar scrub
Mixed with Florida water
And hope

Sleep
Dream
Nightmare
Wake up

Put on my lipstick
Say my prayers
Stretch
Breathe
Drink my water
Do it
All over again

This ritual
Ain't filling my glass
Get me another

Direct Action

I will lay
my saged body
on the front line
for you
reciprocate

For Him

In the unspoken places
You are water
Laughter igniting joy
Pieces of me
Fractals in you

In this darkness
Protected light

Your smell
My familiar
Invites me into you

The smile
I trek back to the day
You first made my blood dance
My heart
Softer

King
You are loved
You are love
You are mine
God…you are mine

Be My Peace

Assumptions of
silence
agreement
balance
for the Black man
no matter his hurricane

It requires [us]
To be the steel basket
Holding
all suffering
Polished
buffed
gleaning at all times
no matter
how heavy
the basket feels
no matter that
the basket
is not steel

but straw

Emasculation

Some men
only want to be emasculated
when it's convenient

Doormat

Your healing
will not be
at the cost
of my back

When He Hurts

Cuts deep
Like the Congo
Precise
Cold blades
Across his spirit

Reactive
Unintentional
None of that matters

I do not recognize me
Daggers flying through my lips
Between purple lipstick

His silence
Burns cigarette holes
In my skin
Misunderstood emotions
You are not unavailable
You don't feel like me
So I make you feel me

I marched
Five steps back
Ten
Twenty
Something like eternity
Will you come and get me?
Walk back into us
Together

Can we
Gently translate
Choreograph
A path
Sway hips
Sway souls
Can I sit
With you
And listen?

Nurturing the Nature of Our Children is Revolutionary.

Our Babies*

I wrote this poem in 2012 after Trayvon Martin was killed. It is as relevant today as it was then.
Our pain is real. And America does not care.

And you thought hope would change it all?
In the moment
when we believed that
we didn't need to
push our Black boys
back into our womb
The beauty of life
that we've been trying
to breathe
into our boys
right after we say
"in spite of...you are..."
What do we tell them now?

justice is
just a
seven-letter word
perfect in ideology
and number
tastes like gunpowder.

In which moment
do we tell them
they can be everything?
When their melanin
boys in blue
and infrastructures
threaten to crush them?

Oh, how can they trust this world
when no education
no "home training"
no prayers
can prepare mamas and daddies
for the phone call?

The girls who love them
left ahead
hoping to birth baby girls
to protect themselves
from this thing
called Black mama pain.
But our girls' life hangs in the balance
This ghost on our shoulders
A teaching moment for my three-year-old daughter
What do I tell her?

Oh, Trayvon!
How I hurt like I knew you
Because I knew you
or some boy
as beautiful as you.
some boy
that made me smile
days before his demise.

Oh, Breonna!
How we fight for you

If history repeats itself
you will keep dying
Some mother
will keep ceasing to be
Some daddy
lucky enough
to make it this far
will keep going numb.

Oh, Michael!
How we'd better keep fighting for you
and each one unnamed
scrubbing away
the blood on those trees
the ghosts of only yesterday
while we keep searching
for that other sun.

A Black Mother's Love

I want to
kegel my babies
back into my womb
place headphones on my belly
play Bob Marley

They can braid each other's hair
I will feed them nothing but green veggies
and strawberries

I will not worry about their hair
not conforming to school standards
They will not see the Black bodies caught on camera
dropping to the ground by a public servant's service

They will not see the worry in my eyes
their father's feverish hands
every time we walk into the world
Together
Alone

The music will drown out
the days when we're called nigger

The times when you're asked to
cut your locs to get a job

That conversation when the police
are called because they thought you
were in the wrong neighborhood

When it is quiet
I will talk with them
about the day
Read books

Ingest honeysuckles
Let the scent creep
through my nostrils
flow down my throat
into my chest
push it down into my belly

I will breathe in the night air
smell the dewy grass
riding on 22s

They will inhale it slowly

They will be warm
placenta-protected
and at peace

Girls Who Know

My ten-year-old daughter asked me about abortion today. The news blared the headline of absurd anti-abortion laws in Alabama. It's 2019 if you're reading this.

"Tell me again, Mom," she pleaded.

When a woman gets pregnant and decides she doesn't want to continue the pregnancy, she can have a procedure to get rid of the pregnancy.

"Okay," she says. "So basically, they don't want it. So a woman can't have an abortion now?"

Yes, that's right.

"But that makes no sense. It's her body. What if she's not ready? What if she just isn't ready? I mean, it's her body, not theirs. So who is anybody to tell her that she can't?"

Exactly!

"What the heck, Mom."

I know.

What Did I Do? My #Blackmommymagic and Overexposing My Babies to Racism

July 7, 2016

I wrote this in March 2016, after a police brutality incident here in Charlotte, North Carolina. Today, I continue to struggle with the preservation of my children in this country, in this world.

As a child, I do not remember a time when I wasn't aware of my Blackness and its implications. Growing up in the 1980s, I was still too young to remember the fight for a nationally recognized MLK holiday. But I remember Stevie Wonder's song playing at home, paying homage to King's life and legacy. Small incidents are etched in my mind, like that Saturday when I was seven, out with my two sisters, two cousins, mom, and aunt shopping at Sears. A little White girl, no older than me, tells her mother, "mommy, I'm surrounded by niggers." I remember my parents' disdain for President Reagan, his racism, and his economic policies. At that age though, I had no deep analysis of the impact of a police state on my Black skin. Not yet.

That is not the case with my seven-year-old daughter. She is unapologetically Black and conscious. Seven and a mere two years old, both of my girls have had their share of rallies, marches, protests, organizing meetings, and legislative sessions. My two-year-old attended her first rally at two months old, strapped across my chest. Awareness is key, right? For my older daughter, she attended her first rally in support of prosecution for the man who killed Trayvon Martin. She was a toddler at the time. Her only real memory are chants of "No justice, no peace." She mostly played with other children on the steps of New Haven City Hall.

But on Friday, March 4, my husband decided to go with me to a protest on the steps of the Charlotte-Mecklenburg Police Department. The protest was organized for a young man who'd been held down by six police officers; one had beat him repeatedly in the head. With no parking in swanky uptown Charlotte, our new hometown, my husband drove around with our two-year-old while I walked to the steps of the police department with our older daughter. Speakers talked about the beating, naming many Black men, women, and children who'd been killed by police. The list went on. An organizer read the list of demands. My daughter asked questions. I obliged.

Then, from a second-floor window of the police building, a police officer peered out of the window. All of us looked up. My daughter looked up for minutes it seemed. She looked at me with the most frightened look I've ever seen and asked quietly, "Does he have a gun? Will he shoot us?" I wanted to say, "Of course not. Don't worry about it. This is our right." But I didn't believe it, and that hurt…deeply. I pulled her close to me, kissed her forehead, held back tears, and whispered, "I hope not, baby. He's just curious. Wants to know what we're saying." It quieted her, but not her fear. It escalated my own uneasiness.

Two minutes later, after listening to a speaker talk about Tamir Rice being killed, my very worried daughter began to cry. "I don't want to hear about this anymore. It's too much death. Why did they kill a boy?" I wiped her tears, hugged her, and told her it was almost over. And it was. In those moments, for the first time in my seven years as a mother, I felt an overwhelming sense of failure. What have I done? Have I gone too far? Does she believe me?

Watching protests on television, protesting on city hall steps, and the conversations at our dinner table were one thing. She was used to hearing her father and me talk about police, incarceration, branding, and the thick atmosphere of racism of the South. But positioning my growing Black daughter on the steps of a police station, in the dark of night, face-to-face with what her father and I had labeled as the nemesis—the police—was a moment I hadn't outlined very well.

We have tried to unpack and analyze for her impressionable mind why a little boy named Tamir Rice had been killed, why people protesting in the streets for Michael Brown was necessary. We've talked about how incarceration still impacts our family, years later. But, in real time, did I put her on the front lines with no bulletproof vest and no mommy assurance? Did I scare her instead of empowering her?

As parents of Black children, there is a necessity in being explicit about how our Blackness is perceived and subjected to surveillance and violence. For some of us, we know that we must prepare them for the attacks, while wrapping them in hope that it will be better for their generation. I am raising Black girls to be conscious, aware, analytical, and proud of their history, beauty, hair, skin, and voice. We read books about history and don't mince words in our home about racism. I strap my babies to my breasts, hold their hand, and walk them along the streets to mobilize them around something they are still struggling to process.

But that night, I failed. My daughter had cried, and her fear was catastrophic. That night, I could not guarantee that she would not be killed or anyone else on those steps. I wiped her tears. She breathed, I held my breath, and we began our walk back to Marshall Park where the group had congregated. With a dry face, she chanted along with us, watched her back, and then stood in the circle for a last prayer and announcements about mobilizing meetings and a Peace Walk the next day. Her smile eased my pain.

As we walked back to the truck where my husband and two-year-old waited hungry and tired, she said to me, "Can I skip Modern and African dance class tomorrow?" "Why?" I asked. "I want to go to the Peace Rally instead," she replied. "I haven't failed!" my mind screamed. "Let's go to dance class. Do what you love." We got in the truck and drove home.

I will not stop taking my girls to rallies and protests. I will not stop them from sitting in on organizing meetings and legislative sessions with other radical babies who sprawled across floors coloring, watching YouTube, or actively listening to the discussions. I will not stop working to tear down systems that were built to destroy my family, my culture, and my people. I will try, however, with vigilance, to give them balance—the balance to fight and to dance.

Generational Wealth

I am grateful
for the **time**
to love on
my children
so slowly
My grandmothers
didn't have space
for it
My mother
created
the door
I open it
usher my children
into the room
My children will
furnish the rooms

The Great Migration

Never been on the L
Traveled to the Chi though
Two times in the city

West side violence they said
We came
for peace

Descended into a
cellar
45 folks in the room
maybe more

Strategized about the violence

Talked healing

What would it look like y'all?

Hit the L
slept for 13 hours…and
That's why i don't hit it

What did i miss?

Count five fingers
two Ls
Can't remember
the other 3

What did i miss?

The L
took me
deep
beyond the Chi
roasting sweet potatoes

The smell
hugging me
Mississippi mud
beneath my feet

AK slung
across my cleavage
Blue daisies
cradle my left arm

Black bubble coat
double dutch rope

Some kid jumped
a turnstile
I got off
looked down

y'all   y'all
it's here
Who knew it would be here
'cuz we suffocated here

Like most migrants
smashed between red bricks

30 to 50
levels of living

Like most migrants
red lines
loud with extraction

Like most migrants
adjust
the hat
recalibrate the skin
for the cold

No red dirt
Familiar mud

Like most migrants

But we're not seen
mislabeled/not
migrant

Floating
Riding
the L
to forget
to not
      remember/I don't remember
what they took

y'all   y'all

Who knew it would drop here
What street is this?
'cuz I don't know the Chi like that

So are we
moving again?

Out of the Chi?
LA?
Minneapolis?
New Haven?
Newark?
Detroit??
Oakland?
St. Louis?

Where else did we run to?

There was message in the L
Said the L showed up
on some corners
       there were seats available
       Some stood
       didn't matter
Folks stomped out their Ls
before they boarded
Didn't need 'em
Not anymore

Stepped in

y'all   y'all

"Doors closing"
the voice blares

Where we going?

To grow sweet potatoes
grease our scalp
Concoct salve
to heal our wrists and ankles
the iron feels
embedded
under my skin
to laugh
in surround sound
in the front yard

We're going to rest
for real this time

Where we going?

To go sign our name
on joy

Being

There are no coupons
to clip
I am at full value
I cash out in gold

Growth

The forgiveness of
my thighs
has expired

Toni Transitions (For the Queen Toni Morrison)

On that morning
a cool breeze passed me
While I painted my toenails blue
No vents were blowing air
No fans spinning
No open doors

I paused
Mid-stroke of my third right toe
smiled…looked up slowly

Hmmm…Good morning, ancestors
That breeze grew cooler
Then walked on
I did not yet know Toni had traveled on

That cool
so familiar
Like the first time I read her words
Like drinking the coldest lemonade
in front of the cleanest mirror

Cries
laughter
anxiety
commonness
sisterhood
resilience
Sula
grief
fierceness
joy
stirring in my bones
Pecola
Realizing my eyes are brown
I am so glad I finally met her
that morning
I cannot wait to talk with her
Conjuring her in this new dimension
I cannot wait to thank her
most definitely
for the cool

Living

Reverence
Discipline
Laughter
Rest
Build a life of words and peace

On Resiliency

I am
Flexible
Amazing
Hard working
Loving
Doing
Imagining
Mothering
Teaching
Wifing
Moving nations
Setting trends

I am
the culture.

I am
Expected
To
Be
It
All
Strong enough
Girl
      Carry on

So I am
Also
Napping
Taking days off
Laughing
Dancing
Pleasuring
Reading
Meditating
Returning

I have endured
I am resilient
I am strong
I am human
I am soft
Welcome to my liberation

Naked

I have never
been this warm
without my clothes
so full of breath
and laughter
Where has this skin been?

She's Here

You are right.
You do not know this her.
But I remember me.
So glad to see her.
Hey boo!

You've Lamented, Now Be Free: An Open Letter to All My Peeps on Your Constructed Doom's Day (Obama Farewell)...and for Today

January 20, 2017

My dear ones,

As a child in the 1980s, living in a musical household with vinyl everywhere, my mother's Minnie Riperton album, *Adventures in Paradise*, became mine. With its grand blue cover, Minnie sat, iconic in a signature '70s cranberry plush chair while petting a massive lion. I played it over and over, singing every word. The album's simplicity was wrapped in songs like "Love and Its Glory," the famous "Inside My Love," and "Simple Things."

Last night in the shower, after being inundated with the many written lamentations and social media posts as President Obama leaves office, and we transition as a country today, the last song of her album, "Don't Let Anyone Bring You Down," entered my spirit. The lyrics are simple:

I'm not gonna sing the blues, 'cause I don't wanna cry. I only wanna be as free as the skies. Don't let anyone bring you down.

There is something about freedom as resistance. As I sang the song over and over, I crafted these words for all of you for today, tomorrow, the next four years, and for your life.

My dear loves,
just be free.
That person is a man.
ONE man.
One set of cabinet cronies
in one cycle of repeated history
Haven't we been here before?

Be free.
Enjoy the quiet
of early morning.
Be free.

Stand as unapologetically Black, Latinx, Asian, Indigenous, Brown, Muslim, Christian, Jewish, spiritual, gay, lesbian, queer, trans, immigrant, undocumented, self-identified self.

Be free.

Don't stand for aggressions.

Learn the political process.

Choose to be a part of it.

Choose to stand outside of it.

Be free.

Be kind and loving.

Stay heightened and awake.

Read. Read. Read.

Be free.

Choose NOT to sit at tables in which you were not a participant in carpentering, and in which you know your presence is not welcome, but tokened.

Choose TO sit at tables in which you were not a participant in carpentering, but do it with intention. Make them accountable for their words, their actions, their beliefs, their history, before you even think about finding common ground.

Build.

Build your community dollars.

See the power of our collectivity.

It's all economic anyway.

Eat dinner around the table with your children.

Talk with them.

Laugh.

Be free.

Do not stand in false solidarity.

Make people accountable for their shit.

Start your education. Finish your education.

Be free.

Acknowledge and capture the wisdom of any elders

with whom you are blessed to share space.

Not everyone has bootstraps.

Let someone grab onto the one you've stitched for yourself.

Be free.

Take care of your body.

*Eat as much clean food as
you can afford and access.
Build across our oppressions.
Be free.
Nurture your children's nature.
Cry.
Give yourself space to heal.
Be free.
NEVER LET ONE PERSON DETERMINE YOUR HAPPINESS.
Be free.
SLAY, even if you're bagging groceries
or cleaning someone's house.
Love is everything.
Be brave.
Be Free. Be free.*

Haiku for All That Is Burning

Ain't enough
books
to analyze this

Crisis KRST COVID

Joy
is what
remains

Hold it
Make love to it
Eat it
Smell it
Dance in it

Consume it
like you did your capitalism
before it left

Nature
is pushing you
to intertwine
to understand its method
to shout out its dopeness

Your resistance
to stillness
is killing you

Silence is deafening
or liberating
Choose your lens

Universe
is calling
on your return
The moon
wants to
dance samba
with you

The sun
wants to smack your ass
into submission

The last shall be first
The first shall be last
The essential
The sacrificed
It is your task to
get all of us
on first

Protection
Love
Joy
is practice

Practice

Your
perfection
is
sustainable

Audacity

Grief met me on the couch
Took my good pillow
Laid its fat ass down
Even farted
Adjusted position
And laid its head
On my chest

Tried to breathe with it
In sync
You know

It weighed more than my frame

I tried to move
Relax my muscles
Get up and walk away

But she's like a bad relationship
With great sex

Gotta shake her off of me

But she's fast asleep
Drooling on my belly button

on the ascension of bell hooks

wednesday, december 15, 2021…11:08 pm

the world feels like less tonight

a hollow shell of itself

i remember lying at your feet
my body wrapped in paper and black ink
drinking you in

today
you are one year older than my mother
a year younger than my father

i feel mortality's wrath

what a year it has been
what a decade we have walked into
there was never enough air
there's never enough air

we try to breathe and every breath is precious
we try to dry out that breath
somehow feel short

space so much of it
not enough of it

the world feels naked tonight
titties hanging

wednesday, december 16th…4:00am Eastern

upon my rising I knew would feel something different
some sort of fullness in this moment
the loss of you

death
introduced you
somebody
maybe didn't know you
until today
       didn't know
              what radical love
                    looks like
                          smells like
                                taste like
                                      feels like.

it jiggles a little
       it dances
              it stretches like putty
                     like the land of our ancestors
                           it bends like my spine
                               its shape shifts
it never pretends
oh, bell.
you keep drawing us into light
new life
new opportunities to walk
to dig deep in the coffers of your words
       to figure out
       to navigate love
       the one thing we want

        the one necessity
        like breath
        that never feels like enough.

i smile
learning to love is mapped
      you smoothed out the cutting edges
          molded them with letters
somebody just discovered you today or
      last night when they heard the news

      somebody discovered themselves

somebody discovered the world
someone discovered the necessity of community
      someone stumbled across the love of intimacy
          somebody somebody's blooming

someone is stretching and winding like the road lit for you to go home

someone is shedding like these leaves outside my window on this warm December morning

        somebody discovered love
             Ase

They Keep Coming for Us

My daughter built a Lego pool

        Mommy let's go to Neptune

I wondered what was there
She wants to be part of the galaxy

And then the news comes on
I turn on the radio
In the car
On the TV
iPad

Pictures of dirty water
Smog
Tears
Blood
Resisting
Resilience

Cycles
Damn near four thousand years old

Broken words
Lies

They say Neptune rains in diamonds

Make it rain
        Diamond showers
                Cold storms
                        Warm winters
Mystery

Go on, baby
Imagine
Dream
Manifest your future

Your destiny

Gimme the green
Red
And black Legos
Let's build

www.ingramcontent.com/pod-product-compliance
Lightning Source LLC
LaVergne TN
LVHW072023060526
838200LV00058B/4657